MORE INSTANT GOLF LESSONS

Published by Golf Digest/Tennis, Inc.
A New York Times Company
495 Westport Avenue
P.O. Box 5350
Norwalk, Connecticut 06856

ISBN: 0-394-75408-5
Library of Congress: 84-63140
9 8 7 6 5 4 3 2
Manufactured in the United States of America

Cover and book design
by Julie W. Francis
Printing and binding
by R. R. Donnelley & Sons

MORE INSTANT GOLF LESSONS

Edited by Peter McCleery

Illustrations by Elmer Wexler, Barbara Morse,
Richard Loomis, Andrew Yelenak, Stan Drake

A GOLF DIGEST Book

CONTENTS

INTRODUCTION

Instant Lessons have been an integral part of GOLF DIGEST'S instruction content for 25 of the 35 years the magazine has been published. Reader surveys have consistently shown that they're the best-read one-page features in any issue; many golfers, it appears, only want or need a simple tip or "key" to get their game back on track.

It is their simplicity, more than anything else, that accounts for the continued popularity of *Instant Lessons,* because with simplicity comes memorability. Of the millions of words we've printed on golf instruction, some of our editors believe that the six used to headline an *Instant Lesson* in August 1975 may have had the most lasting impact: "Swing with ease against a breeze." It is that quality that we have attempted to bring to this book of 100 of the best *Instant Lessons* we've run in the past eight years—an overdue sequel, in fact, to the popular *Instant Golf Lessons,* published in 1978.

There's little chance of misinterpretation with these lessons. Each is graphically illustrated, quick to read and easy to understand. They are written by some of the best-known teachers in the game and reviewed by the instructors of our Golf Digest Schools.

More Instant Golf Lessons is arranged by parts of the game, starting with the setup, progressing into the backswing, forward swing, slicing, sand play, putting—it's all there. Not every tip is going to be helpful to everybody; if you happen to be a hooker, there's not much reason for you to dwell on the slicing section. But you may want to read through the book entirely a first time to pick out those pointers that best meet your needs. Then, when a problem occurs in some phase of your game, you will know where to find an effective cure by referring to the appropriate section.

By far the longest chapter in the book is the 11th—practice drills. This special section gives you proven practice-tee tips on a wide assortment of shots that will help you commit to muscle memory the right moves before you reach the first tee. The concluding chapter, called "Juniors," may actually be mistitled, for these fundamental lessons, although originally written for young golfers, can be equally appropriate to more experienced players who also need to go "back to basics."

Remember that famous antacid commercial, where the low-handicap eater always accepted the waiter's invitation to "try it, you'll like it"? We think it's safe to say "try it, you'll like it" about these tips—for they're almost certain to relieve your game's ailments, not add to them.

—*Peter McCleery*

1 SETUP

Incorporates all the parts you must have in place before you start your address, alignment and ball position.

Check setup with a mirror

Improving your setup position is the easiest way to improve your swing, but any changes at address take a while to adapt to. That's why the winter season is the best time to make a setup change.

Get a photograph, at address, of a touring pro who is similar to you in size and stature, and tape it to a full-length mirror. Then set up with the same club the pro is using and hold your position. Look back and forth between your mirror image and the pro's photo. (Remember, of course, the image will be reversed.) Mentally and physically, make the most obvious correction to look more like the pro. Then walk away and relax for a minute.

Now set up again, employing this new position, and check yourself with the photo. Make one adjustment at a time until you begin to adapt to the pro's position without consciously thinking about all the individual parts.

—*Robert M. Day*

13

Take shoe off to set your weight right

Keeping too much weight on your left side during the backswing causes a reverse weight shift. You'll tend to transfer your weight to the right on the downswing, and lose distance and direction on your shots.

To hit the ball more aggressively, your weight should move from right to left on the downswing—in the direction you're aiming. The easiest way to set up this action is to start with your weight on the right side.

Sometimes exaggeration is the best teacher. I tell my pupils who have trouble experiencing the correct sensation to take off the right shoe in practice. This elevates the left side and accentuates the feeling of weight on the right side.

—*Bud Tonnesen*

Weigh the clubhead before starting swing

Have you ever weighed a golf club? No, I don't mean on a scale. Have you ever weighed a club in your hands? Good players do it all the time. They take their grip, address the ball and slowly waggle the club as if they're trying to feel the weight in the clubhead. This simple, almost unconscious act releases the tension in their arms and prepares their bodies for a full, unrestricted swing.

Some people say, "Keep your arms light." Well, that's not what you're trying to do. Your arms weigh anywhere from seven to 12 pounds apiece. You want to make your arms feel *heavy*—almost like an elephant's trunk when it's swinging.

Next time you're hitting practice shots, try to sense this heavy, relaxed feeling in your arms. When you address the ball, make a slow waggle and *weigh* the clubhead. Don't start your swing until you can feel the weight of the club.

—*Jay Lumpkin*

Focus with left eye to stay behind the ball

A common fault among average golfers is the inability to keep the left side behind the ball on the downswing. Often, the left side slides ahead of the ball, causing the head and shoulders to move and resulting in an off-line shot. Here's how to correct the problem. At address, concentrate on looking with your *left eye* at the *right* side of the ball. Continue to concentrate on this key throughout the swing. You'll be surprised how this simple tip will help you keep the left side behind the ball. Remember: left to right for a truer swing.

—*Paul Miner*

Think of a noose to keep your chin up

I've known golfers over the years who probably deserved to be hanged for their swings, but only once have I resorted to a hangman's noose. The "lynching" occurred when one of my pupils who's also a member of The Golf Club at New Albany, Ohio, came to me for a lesson. His problem was common among average golfers. Trying to keep his head down, he dropped his chin to his chest, tightened his upper body and thereby restricted his shoulder turn.

I asked him if he'd ever seen the noose that hangs from a tree by the 14th hole at The Golf Club, and he had. Then I told him to imagine this noose around his neck as he swung. This image automatically raised his chin at address, allowing his shoulders to turn so that he could make an unrestricted, full swing. Don't put your head in a noose, but think of that image to keep your chin up and lengthen your swing.

—*Bob Ross*

2 GRIP

Placing your hands on the grip properly is the foundation on which a good swing is built.

Double the overlap to add distance

Most golfers use an overlapping grip, with the little finger of the right hand placed over the forefinger of the left hand. I'd like you to try a double-overlapping grip, with the last two fingers of the right hand overlapping the first two fingers of the left. This grip forces you to swing at a pace you can handle. I've found with my students that it improves the timing of the swing and, in most cases, increases distance.

When the hands are spread apart on the club, you generally have more clubhead control but cannot generate as much clubhead speed. The double-overlapping grip, in my view, acts as a more efficient hinge. I recommend it especially to students who have small or weak hands or who have arthritis in the finger joints.

—*Al Wagner*

Wrap a towel around your grip to eliminate tension

Excessive tension in the hands and fore-arms leads to many problems in the swing. A light grip reduces the tendency of the hands to tighten during the swing and thus overcontrol the club. This promotes a better swing pace and an improved swing path. To help my pupils reduce tension, I have them wrap a towel around the grip of the club when they are practicing. This helps them develop trust in a light grip, and a feel for it as well.

—*Chuck Cook*

Rotate left hand to right to kill slice

Many inexperienced golfers hit an abundance of weak, sliced shots. Sometimes, the culprit is a faulty left-hand grip, turned too far to the left. You fit this description if the V formed by your left thumb and forefinger points to your left shoulder. This will cause you to open the clubface and lose clubhead speed through impact, because your hands are not working together.

By turning your left hand more to the right ("strengthening" it) so that the V points between your right shoulder and chin, you'll give yourself a much better chance to square the clubface and increase clubhead speed. Once you have a proper grip, improvement will proceed rapidly.

—Fred Challen

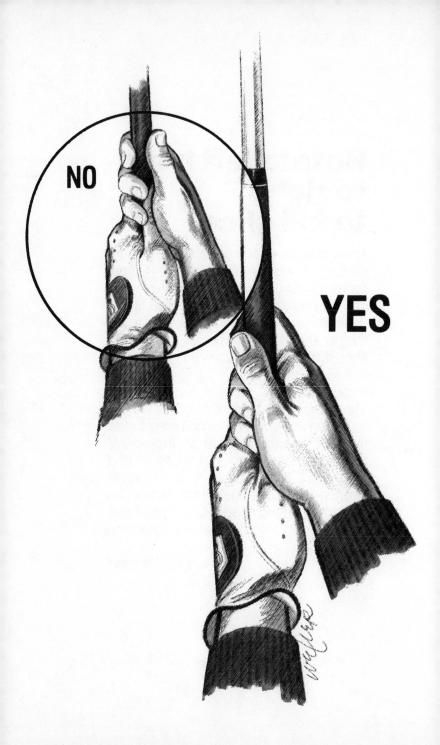

Right thumb should be de-activated

Like many younger players, a student of mine had a very strong grip. The V formed by his right thumb and forefinger pointed to the right of his right shoulder, and his right thumb was positioned down the top-right portion of the shaft. This thumb position caused his entire right side to be overactive, resulting in many hooked shots. To hit the ball straight, he had to "block" the shot, dissipating clubhead speed and destroying distance.

He solved his problems by moving his right hand to the left so the V pointed to the right side of his neck, repositioning his right thumb so it curled partially over the shaft and touched the tip of his right forefinger. His new grip allowed him to release his hands through the ball. He can now hit more aggressively and still get improved direction. Correcting your grip can do that for you.

—John Hinchey

3 BACKSWING

How to begin your takeaway on the right path, achieve a full turn and other swing-starting secrets.

Start your swing with left elbow

A bigger arc usually produces greater distance. But you don't necessarily have to take the club back farther to get a bigger arc. If you lengthen the radius of your swing—the distance from your left shoulder to the clubhead—you will increase the size of your arc.

Try starting the swing with your left elbow. Concentrate on pushing the club back with your left elbow, keeping the clubhead low to the ground at the start. The result should be a bigger arc and more distance.

—Dan K. Howard

Toss a ball to visualize pace of swing

Toss a golf ball up in the air under-handed, coming as close as possible to the ceiling without hitting it. Notice the pace at which the ball rises to the top of its arc, changes direction smoothly, then gradually accelerates downward. Try to think of that as the pace you would swing your arms. Taking the club back too fast is like tossing the ball up in a jerky manner. You'd hit the ceiling and wreck your chances for a smooth transition from backswing to downswing.

Notice also that with a light grip you have maximum control. If you hold on to the ball tightly to toss it up, you have much less control. The same is true in swinging a club.

—*Chris White*

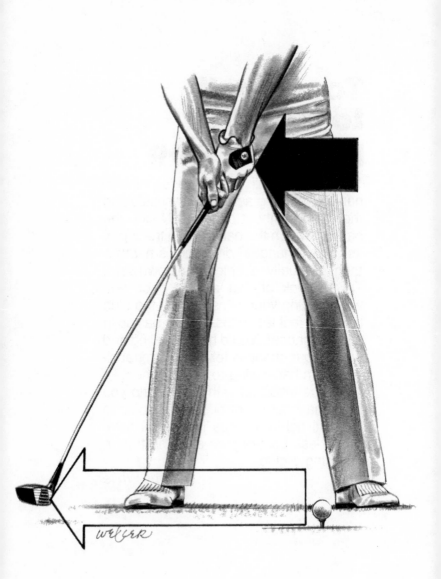

Take clubhead straight back past right foot

A dedicated student of mine was plagued with low, hooking shots because he swung the club around his body in a very flat arc on the backswing, then wheeled the club into the ball with the face closed. He needed a more upright swing, which makes it easier for any golfer to keep the clubface square to the target at impact and hit higher, straighter shots.

I suggested to this student that he start his backswing with a push of his left hand, making certain that the clubhead moved on a straight line directly away from the ball until it passed his right foot. By starting in this manner, he was soon swinging more uprightly and hitting the ball much better—and so will you.

—*William C. Kipple*

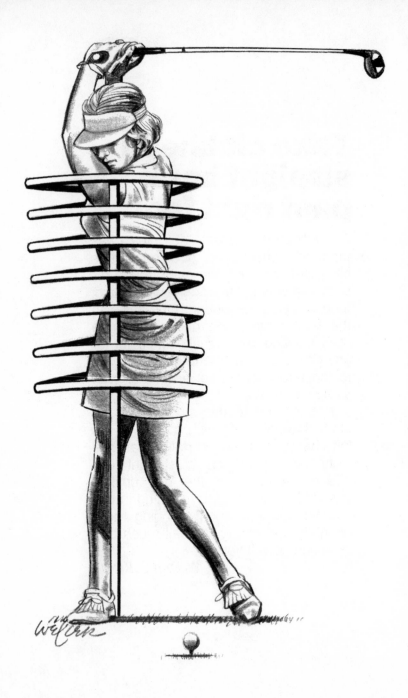

Coil upper body over right leg to cut down tension

Tense golfers cannot swing the club freely, and thus are destined to never reach their playing potential. To reduce your tension level, I suggest you take a lighter grip and let your arms hang freely at address. Then start your backswing with a turn of the shoulders so that your body gradually coils over your right leg. This action properly moves the weight to the right on the backswing and then makes it more natural to move it left on the forward swing.

If too much tension is one of your tendencies, this can go a long way toward reducing it. I had a student practice this and she quickly learned to swing with less tension and added about 20 yards to her average drive.

—*Jimmy Hodges*

Right-hip to left-knee 'rope' teaches aggressive swing

Golfers who can't get a good weight shift to the right on the backswing and to the left on the forward swing can benefit greatly from trying this image: Think of a rope connecting your right hip to your left knee. If you turn correctly on the backswing, the rope will pull your left knee away from the target, your weight will shift to the right and you will be in good position to use the lower body more aggressively on the downswing.

I've found this particularly useful among students whose left knees tend to flex toward the target line with their hips turning very little going back.

—*Fred Phillips*

Imagine force on left elbow starting backswing

You want to have the feeling of beginning the backswing with the arms, not the body. Many golfers have the opposite feeling, with the clubhead lagging behind their hands as they start the swing with a turn of the body. To get it going the right way, I recommend this drill:

Hold the club at address in the left hand only; keeping the back of the hand and wrist straight, turn the club so the grip end points toward the target and cock the wrist. Now imagine a force pushing the left elbow away from the target and swing back easily, not allowing the body to turn until the left hand passes the right leg.

Once you gain the feel of a correct backswing start with this drill, you'll be better able to begin your backswing on a regular basis. With your arms initiating the swing, you'll gain much better distance and control of your shots.

—*Lane T. Creech*

Plant a tee to improve your takeaway

Do you have the common fault of picking up the clubhead on the backswing? It's usually caused by too much tension in the right hand. The ideal starting action is to swing the clubhead low and slow away from the ball, eventually moving it inside the target line. To promote the proper takeaway, I tell my students to stick a tee in the ground approximately 15 to 18 inches behind the ball just inside the target line. As the clubhead is swung away from the ball, it should knock over the tee. When the student feels the click of clubhead against tee on the backswing, he knows he's made the proper takeaway.

—Billy Peterson

Count 'one and two' for better timing

Timing is everything—in golf as in life. A student of mine seemed to be in a hurry to finish her swing from the top. She would not allow her weight to shift to her right side. Well before completing her backswing, with her hands at only shoulder height, she would start her knees toward the target. All this hurt her timing and produced erratic shots.

To improve her timing, I asked her to count "one and . . ." on the backswing, consciously pause at the top and leisurely count "two" before starting down. This slowed and lengthened her backswing, created a better weight transfer and eventually added distance through better timing. If you can count to two, it can work for you, too.

—*Jim Little*

Put clubhead in catcher's mitt to learn proper takeaway

Many players are defeated from the very beginning of the swing because they make an improper takeaway. Being unaware of the feeling of the correct move, they either bring the club back too quickly to the inside, which results in a flat swing, or they take it back too far to the outside, and thus swing too upright. To give a player a mental image of the proper move, I first lay a club on the ground just outside the ball and parallel to the target line. I then ask the player to imagine a baseball catcher crouched down with the mitt in position to catch a pitch about knee high. Now, for the proper takeaway, simply put the head of the club in the mitt. This image encourages the player to take the club straight back and low, with correct left-side extension.

—*Don Trahan*

Cock right knee in to create proper back-swing coil

When your swing is too loose, it causes most of your weight to move to the outside of the right foot during the backswing, creating too much shoulder action coming forward. To tighten this action and create a torque or coil on the backswing, take your address position with your right foot square and your right knee cocked in—toward the target. This teaches you to swing back against a braced right side, retaining the right-knee cock. By setting up this pressure at the top of the swing, your legs will react voluntarily on the forward swing and you'll reduce that excessive shoulder motion.

—*Jackson Bradley*

Lift your heel to start your swing on the right foot

Many weekend players tend to fall back on the follow-through, and this is often caused by starting the takeaway from a "dead" or static position. A simple form of forward press will produce a less complicated—and more effective—swing. Start with your arms loose and limp at address. Waggle the club before beginning your swing. When ready to fire, say to yourself, "And one." On the word "and," raise your right heel off the ground slightly. On the word "one," put your heel back on the ground and begin taking the club back at the same time. Practice this and you'll develop a one-piece arm-and-leg action, resulting in a smoother swing and greater distance.

—*Margo Walden*

Start swing with hip turn to recapture lost distance

When golfers get beyond their 50th birthday, nature begins to take its toll with a variety of ailments that work against a good shoulder and hip turn. To help my senior students recapture the full turn—and the distance it provides —I have them concentrate on starting the swing by turning the right hip away from the ball. This rotation to the right will bring along the left knee and also release the left heel from the ground, making the proper weight shift to the right almost automatic.

—Joe Redanty

4 FORWARD SWING

As you approach the "moment of truth"—impact—these thoughts will help you maximize accuracy and distance.

Point belt buckle at target for accuracy

When you use your hands too much and not enough body to slash at the ball, your accuracy is destined to diminish. To reduce the influence of your hands, think of taking the club back with your shoulders and to swing through the ball so that your belt buckle faces the target at the finish.

With this in mind, your hands should remain relatively inactive and you'll increase the use of your body—along with the accuracy of your shots.

—*Richard Bierken*

Your left hand is the tractor and your right hand the trailer

In the golf swing, I've always believed that your left side must be the leader and your right side the follower. Nowhere is this more true than in the downswing. To generate maximum power and control, your left hand must lead your right hand through the ball.

To illustrate this, I refer to the left hand as the tractor of a tractor-trailer truck and call the right hand the trailer. If the trailer passes the tractor you have an accident on the road or a bad shot in golf. Therefore, you must remember to let your left hand lead even after initial contact is made. This gives you the mobility, momentum and club movement you need.

—*Joe Lazaro*

Hit a home run to learn how to rotate your forearms

Get a baseball bat and take a swing as if you're trying to hit a home run. Hold your position on the follow-through and notice how your forearms have rotated fully. Your follow-through in the golf swing should be very similar.

Now try hitting a home run without rotating your forearms. What probably would result is a pop-up to right field. A golfer with tension in his forearms also cannot get the clubface back to square. The result is golf's answer to a right-field pop-up—the common slice. Keep your forearms free of tension and remember to rotate fully. You'll hit a lot more home runs.

—*Jim Applegate*

Extend left arm like punter's leg for longer shots

Some people fail to achieve sufficient clubhead speed because they "quit" at the ball, with the left arm collapsing through and past the impact area. You can help yourself get up to speed by thinking of the form of a football punter. A punter must fully extend his leg to kick the ball an appreciable distance, and that same thing applies to the left arm in golf through impact. If you practice with this thought in mind, you can increase your clubhead speed and distance —and gain a few more first downs.

—Hugh Moore

Think of a clock to keep swing ticking

I've found in my teaching that relating the swing to a clock face provides a good, simple image for improving both alignment and swing path.

Think of the target as 12 o'clock. Position the ball in the center of the clock face. Then set up along the line that extends from 7 to 11, which is parallel to the target line (6 to 12). The clubface, when placed behind the ball, points to 12.

The path of the arms on the backswing starts toward 6 and then, as the shoulders turn, moves toward 7 and finally approaches 8 as the arms reach their farthest extension at the top.

In your mind's eye, you should try to swing from inside to out toward 1 o'clock on the downswing. This produces a forward swing path that works from inside the target line to along the line to back inside.

—*Sue Keeney*

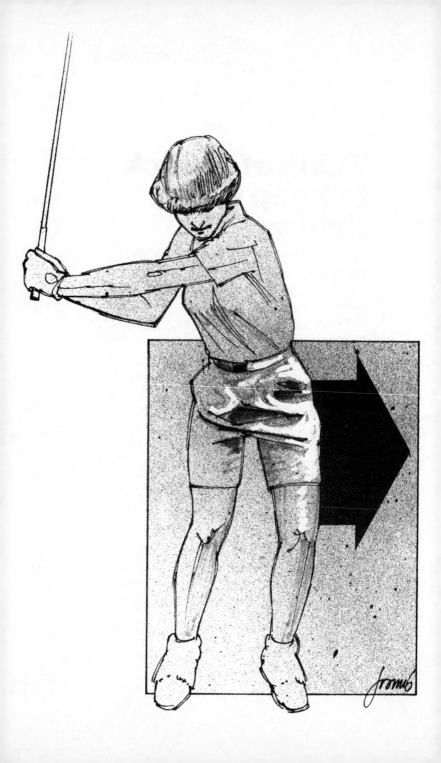

Move hips laterally for more distance

Many new golfers tend to use their hands too soon and their lower body too little in the through-swing. Swinging the clubhead through the ball from outside to inside the target line, these golfers, especially women players, are prone to hitting weak shots to the right.

If this sounds familiar to you, I suggest you forget the hands at the top of the backswing and begin the downward swing with a lateral movement of your hips toward the target. Doing this will help keep your right shoulder from spinning outside, so you will swing the clubhead into the ball from inside the target line. I've found in working with such students that if they try this, they can straighten their shots and add power.

—*Bob Ledbetter*

Think of shooting an arrow to learn proper release

I've found in my teaching that the golf swing is more easily understood when related to other athletic endeavors. My favorite analogy is to an archer shooting an arrow.

The good player feels a buildup of tension on his backswing—a coiling of the hips, shoulders and arms—similar to the tension felt by an archer pulling back a bowstring to shoot an arrow. Once full extension is reached in golf, the body naturally unwinds and the arms and hands swing the clubhead down and through the ball. Likewise, the arrow is released without any conscious effort.

Both are reactions to what has gone before—in golf, the backswing places the club in position at the top, ready to be released—and midway changes are usually futile. Just coil on the backswing and let it happen.

—Gene Miranda

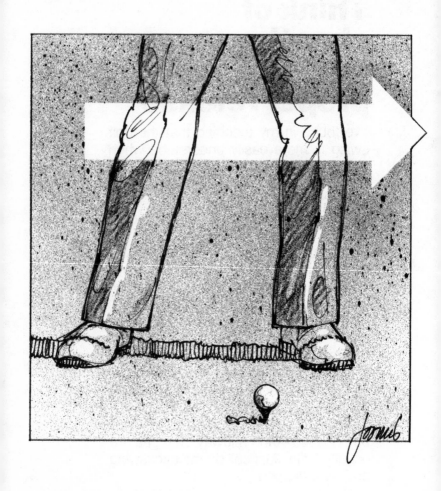

Start forward swing with knees for accuracy

When you swing the clubhead into the ball from outside the target line, it almost invariably causes a pull or a slice. New golfers especially need to understand that you should start the forward swing from the bottom up instead of from the top down.

To build your game properly from the ground up, try starting the forward swing with a movement of both knees toward the target. This will cause the hands to drop straight down and enable you to swing the clubhead into the ball from inside the target line—and start hitting straighter shots.

—Norbert A. Wilson

5 FINISH

Your job isn't done until the follow-through is complete; these "finishing touches" can help you do the job right.

Push your tummy toward the target

Most of us have been told at one time or another to "pull in that tummy." The reverse advice—"push out your tummy"—can help your golf swing.

Try pushing your midsection toward the target on your follow-through. This move has a couple of benefits: (1) you will turn your hips through the ball and generate more powerful leg action, and (2) your body will finish in the reverse C position, insuring a full, unrestricted follow-through.

—*Richard T. Mackey*

To follow through fully, think of posing for a picture

A proper transfer of weight is essential to a sound swing. You should finish with the weight on your front foot, your belt buckle facing the target, your hands high and the sole of your right shoe facing away from the target. To help you get there, before your shot think of yourself posing in the follow-through position—as if someone were taking your picture.

—Mark King

Finish like a pro to promote balance

One thing all good golf swings have in common is balance. Every good player I've ever seen has swung the club in balance—finishing in a relaxed follow-through position, watching the ball fly toward the target. To promote good balance I tell my students to bring the arms and hands back down after the follow-through and hold them waist high, with the club pointing straight up. This thought encourages you to swing the club away smoothly on the backswing and maintain your balance on the down-swing. It also improves your swing plane. Watch the touring pros on television and you'll see that many of them finish their swings in this manner. It's worth a try.

—Jim McLean

Drive through finish tape for proper weight transfer

The average golfer does not make a proper weight transfer to his left side on the downswing. To develop an image of this movement, imagine a finish-line tape just in front of your left thigh at address. Now try to break the tape as you drive your legs through impact and on into the follow-through. Remember, break the tape with your thigh—not your upper body, which should remain basically behind the ball as you swing through.

—*Ted Hopkins*

Straight-up finish for straighter shots

I had a student who had reached his plateau as a player a few years back, and it was obvious he could not improve any further until he cured his bad habit of duck hooking. The problem was due to his reaching impact too late in his swing, at a point when the clubface was closing instead of square. The student was sliding his hips toward the target through the ball instead of turning them. It resulted in a severe reverse C finish, with the center of his body extended farther along the target line than his upper body.

I told him to think about finishing in a more erect and balanced position, with his right shoulder directly over his left foot. Aiming for this position induced the student to reach the ball slightly earlier in his swing, when the clubface was still square to his target line. This procedure eliminated that nasty duck hook.

—David Horn

6 SLICING

Proven cures for golf's most common problem—the distance-robbing "banana ball."

Stop slicing by swinging to the right

Clubhead path—swinging from outside to inside the target line through impact—is largely responsible for slicing. Such a path imparts left-to-right sidespin to the ball. To hit your shots straighter, you need to swing the clubhead straight down the target line.

To teach this, I sometimes place a wooden tee in the turf two feet past the ball and four inches to the right of the line, then ask the student to swing an 8-iron so that the clubhead passes over that tee. As you move to longer clubs, position the intermediate target farther down the line, finally placing a towel 10 feet past the ball and a foot to the right of the line for your driver.

This will effectively change the curvature of your shots so that you'll hit a slight draw as your inside-out swing imparts right-to-left spin.

—Ken Lindsay

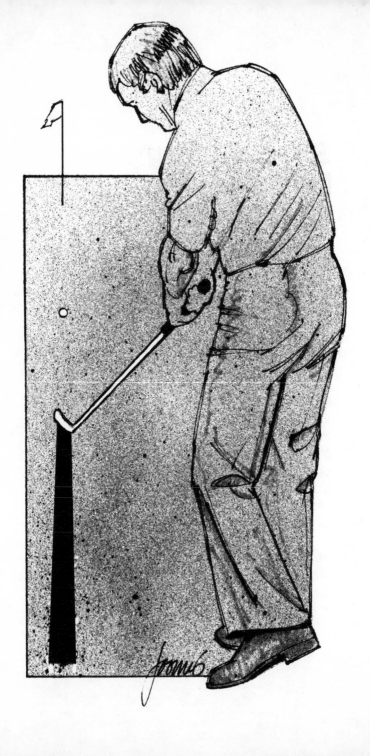

Extend arms to end slice

I had a slicer who started the clubhead back outside the target line and came into the ball on the same line. He asked me how he could cure the problem. I told him to think of swinging the clubhead straight back and through with extended arms. He soon was swinging down from inside the target line and hitting much straighter shots. His outside-to-inside clubhead path was corrected and his slice was eliminated.

By thinking of extending your arms in this way, you can straighten out your shots, too.

—*Nino DelGado*

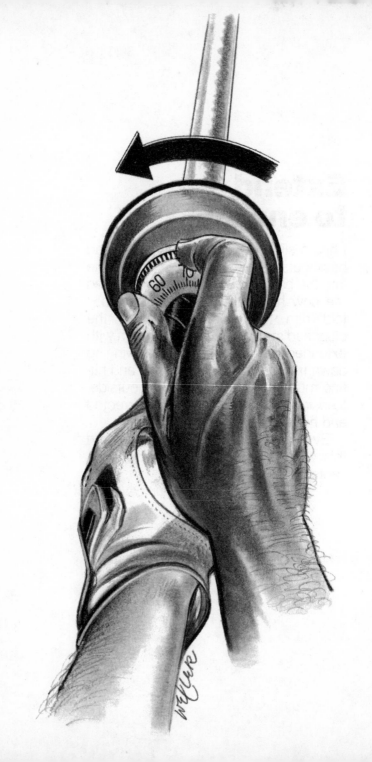

Turn up a thermostat to release

One reason golfers slice is because they don't release through the ball. That is, they don't allow the forearms and hands to rotate in a counterclockwise direction on the downswing, which squares the clubface at impact. To achieve the proper release, think of the motion needed to turn up a thermostat. Make a conscious effort to perform this simple counterclockwise movement of the hands and forearms every time you swing and you'll find your shots going straighter—and longer.

—Keith Brady

Keep right elbow in front of right hand for proper approach

There are many misconceptions about the role of the arms in the golf swing, and I have a simple key that helps eliminate confusion in the mind of my pupils. I tell them to keep the right elbow in front of the right hand in the early stages of the downswing. This method keeps the right shoulder back and assures that the clubhead approaches the ball from inside the target line. When the right hand gets ahead of the elbow too soon, it means the clubhead will approach the ball from outside-to-inside, resulting in a pull or pull slice.

—*Art Schilling*

Straight left wrist at top does the trick

A chronic slicer's problem was traced to an open clubface at impact. Actually, she opened the clubface during the backswing, cupping her left wrist at the top. The clubface pointed more or less vertically at that point and she was unable to square it at impact.

To help her square the face so that it would make contact aiming at the target, I asked her to think of a splint being on the back of her left wrist so that it would remain straight throughout the swing. This squares the clubface—it points upward at a 45-degree angle at the top—and it will stay square through impact if this wrist position is maintained.

—*Gary Toulson*

'Stick your club in the mud' to cure a slice

A slice—when the ball curves from left to right (for a right-handed player)—is caused, at least in part, by an open clubface at impact. When the clubface is open, it is aimed to the right of the target. To eliminate an open clubface, imagine a mud bank directly in front of the ball and try to stick the toe of the club into that mud bank. Soon your shots will be flying straight or hooking slightly from right to left, which will give you added distance.

—Chuck Cook

7 PUTTING

Tom Watson says it's half the game, and there's no doubt about the stroke-saving potential of good putting.

Putt short ones with authority

In putting the short ones, be sure to strike the ball firmly. Many short putts are missed because the stroke is tentative and the ball is pushed rather than struck. Think of a Marine drill sergeant and stroke the short putts with authority.
—*J.M. (Johnny) Anderson*

Sight the target down a 'gun barrel'

Setting up for putts so that your head and eyes are behind the ball will give you a better perspective and help you to stroke the ball smoothly. Think of sighting down a gun barrel to make sure you are looking down the target line from behind the ball.

—Jeff Burey

Aim your short putts at a blade of grass

On short putts, don't just aim at the hole. Pick out a blade or tuft of grass on the back edge of the cup and zero in on that point. Forget about the hole and concentrate on that single blade of grass as your target.

—*Robert Becker*

Keep your eyes on the hole to improve feel for distance

I've found that most golfers have trouble with long putts because they don't let the putter swing freely. They tend to have a short backswing and they over-accelerate through the ball, breeding erratic rhythm and inconsistent results.

One good drill I recommend to improve feel for distance is to look at the hole while you putt. That's right. Focus your eyes on the target at address and keep them there when hitting the ball. Feel the putter swing back and through like a pendulum, changing direction at the same speed. Practice this on the putting green from about 10 feet and then gradually work back to longer putts. This drill helps you use your eyes better to judge distance and teaches you to trust what you feel.

—David Glenz

Pack a tent to read strange greens

Your imagination can help you save strokes when you're putting on unfamiliar greens. Putts that apparently break in one direction often break just the opposite way because your eyes are deceived by the surrounding terrain.

Imagine that you're walking into a tent that covers the entire green as you approach it. Cup your hands over your eyes to help form the tent in your mind. With outside distractions gone, the real slope and roll of the green will be more obvious.

This cover-up tactic should help you reduce three-putting on courses you're playing for the first time.

—Larry Crawford

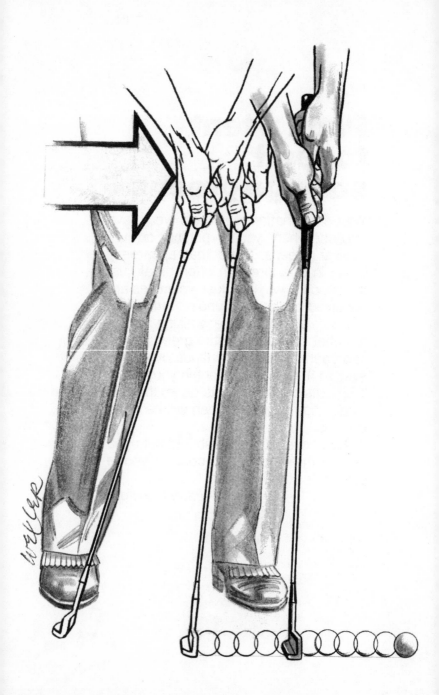

To accelerate putterhead, move handle past left knee

Most inconsistent putting is the result of the putterhead decelerating as it strikes the ball. If the arms slow down, or stop in the impact area, the left wrist collapses and the putterface tends to twist open or closed. This problem is especially common on short putts you *have* to make. Just think of moving the handle of the club toward the target and past the left knee. This helps you accelerate the putterhead through the ball, insuring solid contact and more consistent putting.

—*Jimmy Hodges*

Open stance to improve your putting perspective

There is an increasing tendency among good putters today to putt with an open stance. Most notably, Lee Trevino and Jack Nicklaus address their putts with their feet aligned to the left of the hole. And certainly Sam Snead, with his sidesaddle technique, faces the hole when putting. While there are still many good players who use a square setup, I think open-stance putters have several advantages. First, aligning to the left gives you a better perspective of the target. An open stance allows you to set your eyes on the target line but behind the ball, which improves your aim and feel for distance. It also helps you swing the putter low to the ground, eliminating one of the most common faults of poor putters—picking up the putterhead abruptly on the backswing.

—*Tom Nieporte*

Close your eyes to improve putting feel

There are almost as many putting styles as there are golfers. However, two basic fundamentals that most excellent putters employ are (1) very light grip pressure, and (2) equal speed and length of the backswing and forward swing. With these two thoughts in mind (and in hand), proceed to the practice green and close your eyes the instant you strike the first putt. Now, with eyes still closed, and relying strictly on how the putt *felt,* determine if the ball is right or left and long or short of the hole. Continue to close your eyes on each putt, estimate the result, then check your judgment. By practicing this, and varying the distances, you will surprise yourself with rapidly improved putting.

—*Jerry Holley*

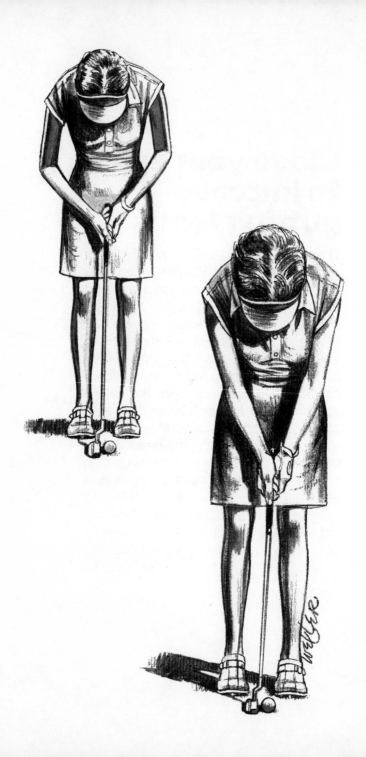

Cut off your putter to cut off strokes

Many persons putt poorly simply because they use a putter that is too long. This causes them to set up with a "broken" left wrist and with the arms so bent at the elbows that the arms and shoulders cannot swing freely along the target line. By simply shortening the puttershaft you will be able to set up with extended arms and a flat left wrist. To determine your correct shaft length, assume your normal putting posture and let the arms hang naturally. Grip the putter where your hands fall. Now have your pro or someone at a club repair shop cut off the portion that extends above your hands and have a new grip put on. Skirts and slacks don't come in the correct length for everyone—and neither do putters.

—*Sue Keeney*

Putt fast downhillers off toe of blade

A downhill putt on a fast green presents a special problem. You must not hit the ball too hard, yet you want to make a smooth stroke. To make sure the ball does not jump off the putter too quickly and roll far past the hole, line it up and strike it with the toe of the blade. You will take enough impetus off the putt to roll the ball slowly down the hill.

—*Jim Lucius*

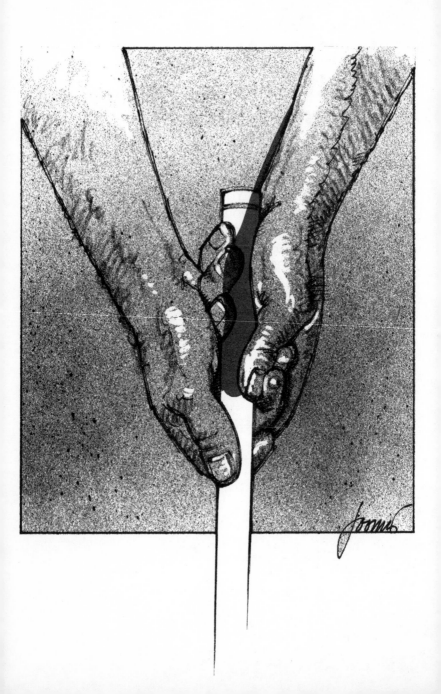

Turn left thumb to 10 o'clock for wristless putting stroke

A too-wristy putting stroke will often cause a pupil to miss putts to the right. A simple adjustment of the grip can often remedy the problem. Move your left thumb counterclockwise from the top of the shaft to a "10 o'clock" position, placing the left hand more under the shaft.

With this change, you can adopt a wristless, pendulum putting stroke that will move the putterhead straight through the ball on the target line.

—*Frank Herrelko*

8 PITCHING & CHIPPING

Ace short-game advice that can help you get "up and down" from off the green more often.

Accelerate the clubhead like a roller coaster for high pitch shots

To hit the pitch shot with a high trajectory, think of the action of a roller coaster at an amusement park. Take the club up at a slightly sharper angle than normal on the backswing and then let the weight of the clubhead accelerate through the ball on the downswing, like the roller coaster heading down. Make sure you follow through and finish high.

—*J.M. (Johnny) Anderson*

Get the right heel up on chips and pitches

When playing a routine pitch or chip shot to the green, golfers often find themselves hitting the ball fat and well short of the target or skulling it over the green. The reason this happens is that the clubhead gets ahead of the hands before impact.

To avoid these mis-hits, address the ball with your hands preset in front of the clubhead and your weight predominantly on the left side. During the downswing make sure your right heel lifts off the ground, and on the follow-through balance yourself on the big toe of your right foot. This swing thought encourages you to hit down on the ball with your hands leading the clubhead.

—*John M. Kennedy*

Use an extra ball to fine-tune your short game

Many golfers have the idea that they should *scoop* the ball to get it airborne on chips and pitch shots. They drag the clubhead back low to the ground and then make a sweeping hit. This often results in fat or topped shots.

The most effective chipping or pitching technique is to strike down on the ball. But many players can't strike *down* because they never get the clubhead *up* on the downswing.

I've found the best method of practicing a descending blow is with a spare ball positioned about eight or nine inches behind the ball you intend to hit. This forces you to swing the clubhead up on the backswing and hit down on the ball sharply with the forward swing. Remember, you can't strike *down* unless the clubhead first goes *up*.

—*Dale Mead*

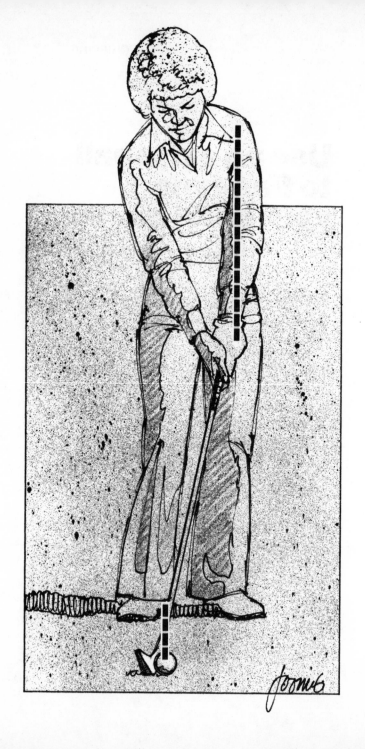

Ball back, hands under your left shoulder for better chipping

Inability to chip decently has spoiled many a decent ball-striker's scores. A lot of poor chippers play the ball too much off the left foot, use a wristy stroke and mis-hit their short shots.

A readjustment of your stance can help you hit low, running chips that consistently finish closer to the cup. Use a slightly open stance, play the ball off your right heel and position the grip end of the club directly below your left shoulder. Using a shorter, firmer stroke with no wrist break, you'll be able to achieve crisp contact much more consistently—and thus save a lot of strokes around the green.

—*Denny Miller*

Use the 'triangle' for pitch and run

When you are faced with a pitch-and-run shot, you don't want to break the wrists because that will create backspin, stopping the ball short of the target. Start the takeaway with the shoulders and leave the hands and wrists as a single unit on the club. Think of the shoulders, arms and hands as a triangle. Start with the hands slightly ahead of the ball at address and, using the triangle, stroke the ball firmly one-third of the distance to the hole with a 7-iron. The ball will land softly with very little spin and will roll the other two-thirds of the way. Remember also not to break the wrists on the follow-through. Just let the triangle do the work.

—*Ron Jensen*

Perfect your pitch shots with the 'mini swing'

The pitch shot is performed by using either a pitching wedge or a sand wedge and a portion of the full swing. Beginning golfers can learn how to control the direction and trajectory of this shot by practicing what I call the "mini swing." The alignment of your body must be parallel to your target line and the club-face set squarely on that line—and the club must swing from inside to along the target line to produce a straight shot. Relax your hands and forearms so that you can feel the weight of the clubhead. After making a backswing that relates in length to the distance of the shot, let gravity cause the clubhead to drop to the ground so contact is made at the bottom of the golf ball.

—*Kathy Murphy*

NO

YES

Use a broom to brush up short-game stroke

By practicing your putting and chipping strokes with a broom, you can eliminate excess wrist action and sweep away your short-game shortcomings. Take a broom and grip it one-half to two-thirds down the handle. Put the top part of the broom handle under your target-side arm; angle the broom if you are going to "chip," set it more upright if you plan to "putt." Now make your stroke. If you are producing the correct movement, you will feel the target-side arm pulling the broom through the hitting area, and the handle will remain in place. If you are using too much wrist action, the broom handle will crack you in the ribs.

—*Gretchen Byrd*

9 SAND PLAY

"The scariest shot in golf" can become one of the simplest if you follow these suggestions.

Listen for the pebbles playing out of sand

Your preswing thought on greenside bunker shots should be to hear the sand splashing on the green. This helps you pinpoint your concentration and keep your upper body steady as you swing through the shot. It also helps you gauge how hard to swing, because if you can get the sand pebbles on the putting surface, the ball usually will finish there, too.

—*Gene Lesch*

Blast a pancake out of the bunker

I have yet to find a golfer who practices greenside bunker shots without a ball— and that's really one of the best ways to learn to play out of sand. With the blade slightly open, take several full swings and blast sand out of the bunker. Try to *feel* the softness of the clubhead bouncing through the sand.

Next draw a circle in the sand about the size of a small pancake, maybe four or five inches in diameter. Shuffle your feet to get a firm footing, address the "pancake" as you would a ball and make a full swing at a moderate pace. The idea is to hit the whole pancake out of the bunker.

Finally, try it with a ball in the center of the circle, like a dab of butter on a pancake. Concentrating on displacing the whole area of the pancake with the clubhead will help you consistently get the ball out and closer to the hole.

—*Jim Silvey*

Keep weight on left foot to get out of bunkers

The biggest mistake most golfers make in the sand is trying to lift the ball out of a bunker by staying on the right foot and swinging the club at the ball. When this happens you will hit too far behind the ball and leave it in the bunker, or you will hit the middle of the ball and send it over the green. Set up to the ball with your feet at about 45 degrees to the target line, your weight mostly on your left foot. Then take the club back as naturally as possible and hit down and through the sand underneath the ball while your weight stays left. Keeping your weight on the left foot allows you to relax and know that the ball is going to get out of the bunker and onto the green.

—*Bill Garrett*

Watch flying sand for better bunker play

I once had a student who was so shaky from the sand that he always chipped out, not even trying to use a sand wedge. Later, when he first tried the sand wedge, he often stuck the clubhead deep into the sand and left the ball in the bunker. Now he is so accomplished that he gets up and down in two from greenside bunkers more often than many golfers with lower handicaps.

The simple thought of watching for flying sand after impact helped him master this shot. Cutting a shallow divot, the clubhead sliding smoothly under the ball, is an integral part of good sand play. The clubface must stay open, so the flange or "bounce" rides through the sand, or it will dig in too deeply. When you can see the sand fly, you know you've performed a dandy "sandy."

—*Nick Andrakin*

Grip with clubface open for sand and cut shots

Two shots that give golfers more trouble than they should are the sand shot and the cut shot. The principle behind both is the same: you must hit the shot with the clubface open to pop the ball up and out. Most players try to open the clubface by rolling their hands on the backswing or by opening the face at address after taking their grip. Rather than rolling your hands, first set the clubface open. Only then finalize your regular grip and stance. Proceed with your normal swing, and the clubface will remain open throughout the entire shot.

—*Mike Limback*

Use a board to feel 'bounce'

A proper sand club is one of the keys to effective sand play. A well-designed sand club has an inverted flange (the back of the sole is lower than the front) so that on normal greenside bunker shots, the trailing edge of the flange will help the club bounce through the sand underneath the ball.

To feel the club bouncing through the sand, try this practice drill: Place a three-foot 2 x 4 board in the sand. First, make a few swings just bouncing the club off the top of the board. Then add a one- or two-inch layer of sand to the middle of the board and bounce the club off the board again, displacing the sand. Finally, put a ball on the sand on top of the board, and again bounce the club off the board to displace the sand, which in turn displaces the ball.

—*Andy Nusbaum*

10 SPECIALTY SHOTS

A selection of shots that come in handy on certain "special occasions."

Keep your hands on the table to hit it low

When hitting into the wind or under tree limbs, you need to keep the clubhead traveling on as low and level a path as possible. Imagine at address that you're set up alongside a table. As you swing, picture your hands staying on the table top as the clubhead passes through the ball. This image promotes a level angle of approach and low shot trajectory.

—*J. Rodney Loesch*

Practice off a board to learn wood shots from bare lies

Many golfers are reluctant to hit wood shots from bare lies, fearful they will hurt their hands or damage the club. To overcome that fear, practice hitting the ball from a wooden board, using a smooth sweeping motion and trusting the loft of the club to get the ball airborne. Outside of a scratched soleplate, I've never heard of anyone hurting himself or damaging a club using the drill. You'll be amazed what it can do for your confidence the next time you're confronted by a shot from hardpan, a close-cropped fairway or even a sand trap.

—*Carl Gallo*

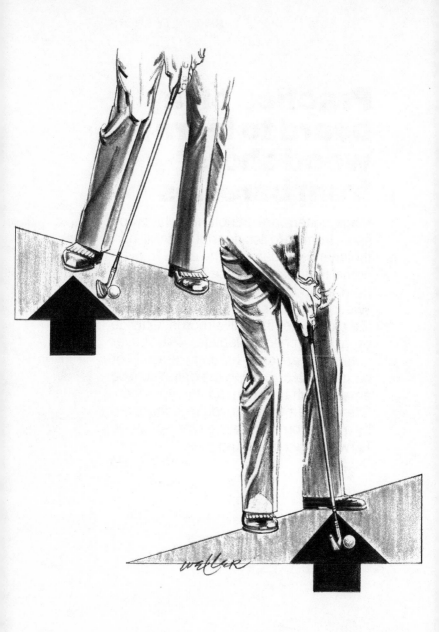

Play ball toward higher foot on uphill and downhill lies

Ball position is vital to getting the ball airborne from uphill and downhill lies. A good rule of thumb is to always move the ball toward your higher foot. On an uphill lie the ball should be positioned toward your left foot, which is your highest foot as you stand on the slope. On a downhill lie the ball should be moved toward your right foot, which again is your highest foot when faced with this shot. Keep in mind that, as a result of your stance, you're likely to fade the ball downhill and draw it uphill, so aim accordingly.

—*Jock Olson*

Use preset swing close to obstacle

When your ball comes to rest near an obstacle such as a tree, bush, fence or large rock and you have little room to make a backswing, this specialty shot is a great stroke-saver. It will work with as little as six inches of backswing, enabling you to get out of trouble without taking a penalty drop that still might leave you in bad shape. The procedure:

• Use a wedge or other lofted club because you will be striking sharply down on the ball and taking loft off the club.

• Take a preset position with your hands about in the impact position and your wrists fully cocked.

• Set the clubhead against the object that is restricting your swing.

• When you are ready to hit, simply snap your wrists and release the clubhead into the ball.

—*Hal Morrison*

11 PRACTICE DRILLS

A special section of practice-tee tips covering all aspects of the game. By doing drills related to your game's needs, you'll train yourself to make the right move when it counts on the course.

Swing with 'wrong' end to improve balance

To build better balance in your swing and promote a more complete follow-through, try warming up with this practice drill. Grip the club at the "wrong" end—by the hosel—and take a full swing. It might feel a little awkward at first, but practicing with this drill helps you increase arm speed. On the practice tee, hit all your clubs with the same procedure: drill, shot, drill, shot. This exercise also helps you accelerate with your left arm, swinging *through* the ball and not simply *to* it.

—Don Pender

Right-handed golfers should become lefties in other things

If you are a right-handed golfer, get in the habit of doing other things left-handed. The most common fault of right-handed players is their inability to use the left hand, arm and side in the golf swing. You can build up your left-side strength and dexterity by using the left hand more often.

Learn to do a variety of things with your left hand—for instance, teeing up your ball, pulling your golf cart, pulling your clubs out of the bag, brushing your teeth and, even, eating and drinking. The more you become left-side conscious, the better your left side will work in the golf swing.

—Gene Dixon

Split-handed drill teaches weight shift

Golfers who find it difficult to learn the feel of a good weight shift and who don't use their legs properly may profit from this drill: Take a normal stance and hold a club at both ends, the sole pointing at the target. The left hand should be on top of the clubhead end and the right hand under the shaft on the grip end. Now swing back until the clubshaft is perpendicular to the ground.

This drill forces a person to make the correct swing moves, even in slow motion. By doing this exercise, the feeling of shifting your weight back and forth will become ingrained and you'll be able to apply it to your regular golf swing with ease and effectiveness.

—Jerry Claussen

Reverse swing to loosen up on the first tee

If you don't have time to hit balls before a round of golf, you should perform some form of exercise on the first tee to loosen up your muscles and reacquaint them with the motion of the swing. I've found the easiest way to relax tight muscles is to make a dozen practice swings from the "wrong" side—if you're right-handed swing left-handed, and if you're left-handed swing right-handed. Then take a few practice swings from the "correct" side and play away. This exercise stretches the lead hand, arm and shoulder muscles, and improves your chances for a free, unrestricted turn on the early holes.

—*Mike Calbot*

Practice foot-line drill to improve swing path

Here's a practice drill that I teach the junior golfers at my club, but it will work for players of all ages. I call it the "foot-line drill," because the right foot is placed directly in line behind the left at address. When you swing, keep your feet in this position and try not to fall off balance. This setup instinctively promotes: (1) the proper takeaway path to the inside of the target line; (2) the proper arm swing and clubhead path from inside to out through impact; (3) the proper forearm rotation throughout the swing; (4) good balance and rhythm, and (5) hand, eye and ball coordination.

—*Don Kotnik*

Think 'driver' in sand—and vice versa—for better tempo

Too many golfers get into trouble because they have two different swings —neither of them suitable for the shot at hand. For example, the golfer is likely to overswing with the driver, then make a short, quick swing with his sand wedge. The ideal situation is one in which the golfer reverses his thinking, so that he takes a shorter, more controlled swing with the driver and a fuller, slower swing with the sand wedge. Try it the next time you play or practice and you'll get improved results both off the tee and from the sand.

—*Ed Kelly*

Visualize your favorite pro

While the golf swing is an act performed mechanically by your muscles, all that motion—conscious and subconscious —is controlled by your mind. That's why you occasionally amaze yourself by hitting a great recovery shot; you are able to stimulate your imagination to the degree that you can visualize the exact flight of the ball from trouble to safety. To activate this ability to visualize, simply picture in your mind your favorite pro making a perfect swing. Try to let your imagination sense the power and rhythm of the stroke as well as the path of the swing itself. Now play your shot and just try to mirror your own imagination. It takes practice, but soon you can see yourself hitting the same great shots as your favorite pro. An added benefit to this mental drill is that when you are visualizing positively, there is no opportunity to think negatively.

—Al Gerring

Forget target when practicing short shots

Taking your eyes off the ball on the backswing is one of the major causes of missed shots in the short game. Once the eyes "lose sight" of the ball, the hands react by "groping," the wrists break too early on the downswing and the clubhead hits behind the ball. To solve the problem, hit 30 or 40 practice shots around the green without regard to the target. Don't even look up to see how each shot finishes. Just discipline your mind and body to concentrate on the ball, and strive for solid contact. Only after that is achieved should you worry about distance.

—Kyle Burton

Swing with the left arm only to develop control

Tennis players often lose direction of their golf shots due to overuse of the right hand, arm and side in the down-swing. To increase the accuracy of their golf shots, these people need to develop strong left-side control.

To induce this control, I suggest students practice hitting shots using only the left arm. Some accomplished male athletes I've taught soon find they can hit a 7-iron shot 100 yards this way, and it becomes clear to them that the left side plays an all-important part in the golf swing.

When you return to placing two hands on the club, you should retain control of the swing with the left side, especially at the start of the forward swing. The right side's strength comes into play through impact naturally, without special thought or effort, and you'll hit a lot fewer off-line shots.

—*Roger Jones*

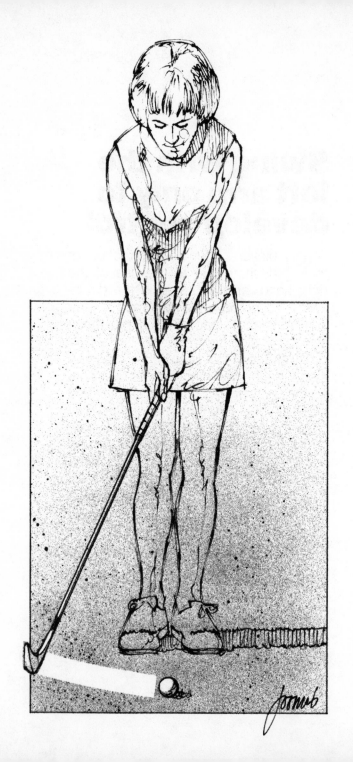

Eliminate swaying with this feet-together drill

Swaying almost always leads to an inconsistent swing and inconsistent shots. In an effort to move her weight to the right side on the backswing, I had a woman student recently who would usually sway her hips away from the target.

To help her learn the feeling of a proper shoulder turn and weight shift, I gave her this drill: With the feet close together, start the club back with only the hands, arms and shoulders, not consciously thinking of any weight shift.

Gradually moving her feet farther apart (finally to full-swing position), this student eliminated her hip sway, began turning her shoulders and prevented her weight from moving to the outside of her right foot. Try it to chase your sway away.

—*Gene Diamond*

Practice those short putts with tennis balls

Most missed short putts are the result of anxiety or lack of confidence rather than mechanics. At those times the hole may appear small and remote. A simple yet effective way to overcome this and create confidence in your stroke is to practice putting with tennis balls. Take two tennis balls and two golf balls to the putting green and start with the tennis balls. Stand one putter length away from the hole and stroke the oversized balls toward the hole until you sink five in a row. If you miss, start over. After you've aced your fifth consecutive tennis ball, put the tennis balls aside and putt with the golf balls. The ball will seem like a marble and the hole a bucket. You'll sink a lot more of those three- and four-footers.

—*Rick Vershure*

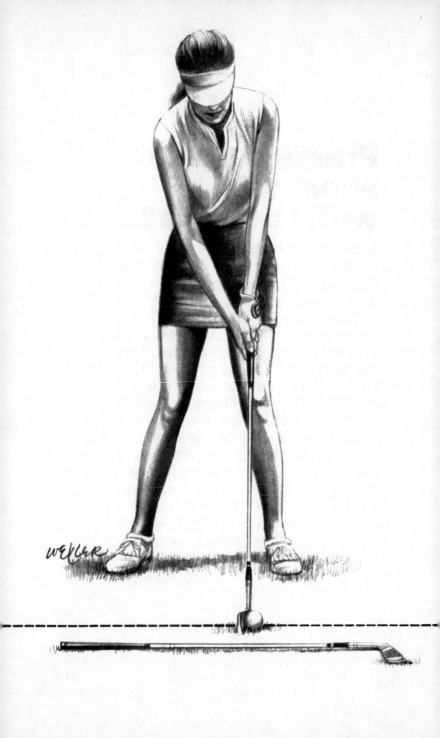

Practice with pointer club to align correctly

Even players as accomplished as Jack Nicklaus and Tom Watson still use a pointer club on the practice tee. So should you to develop proper alignment. Placing the club on the ground next to the ball and pointing along the target line will give you a closer point of reference to help square the clubface and position your body so that your feet, hips, shoulders and eyes are aligned parallel to the target line.

—Deborah Bond

Use ball-curve drill to learn the breaks

To learn how to handle breaking putts, use this drill. Pick an area on the practice green that gives you a breaking putt of about 20 feet. Try to visualize the line of the putt and place 10 or 12 balls along that line, the first one a foot from the cup and each successive ball about 18 inches back. Putt the first ball into the cup, then putt each successive ball over the spot where the previous ball lay, giving it the speed that would let it die into the hole. You can mark where each ball was by a spot on the green or with a coin set just to one side of it. Remember, you are putting over each previous spot with the correct speed, not necessarily trying to make the putt. When you get to the last ball, decide whether your line was good or bad, then try to make the final putt. This drill soon will sharpen your judgment.

—*Peter Kostis*

Hit practice shots specific distances

To make your practice more productive, hit your shots to a target at a specific distance rather than just launching them into the blue. For example, if you hit 5-iron shots 140 yards, visualize an imaginary flag at that distance and direct your shots to it. This kind of visualization will give you a better swing feel for both direction and distance, and you will be better prepared for the shot when you get on the course. Also you will be less prone to try to get more distance out of the club than is comfortable.

—John Elliott

Measure your putting stroke with a pair of yardsticks

Good putters generally have firm, short putting strokes. The golfer who allows his backstroke to get too long runs the risk of decelerating through the ball. When the putter slows down, the hands take over and twist the clubface off-line.

If your putting needs help, concentrate on making a firm, short stroke. Spend more time practicing straight putts of three to five feet. I have my students practice with two yardsticks— one placed to the outside of the putting line and the other to the inside. The yardsticks immediately improve alignment. They also help keep the putter-face square to the target line, which is desirable, especially on short putts.

When practicing with the yardsticks, remember to keep the backstroke relatively short and accelerate smoothly. Think "firm and short" and you'll make more putts.

—*Kelley Moser*

197

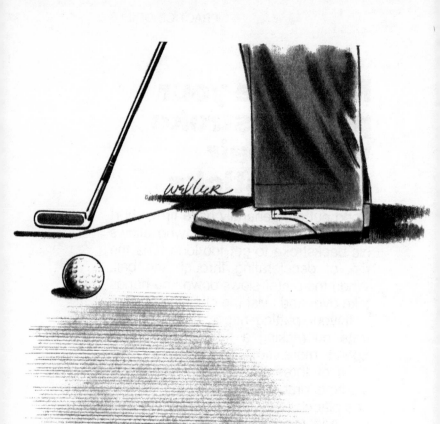

Make target smaller and hole larger number of putts

A good drill to sharpen your putting is to use a smaller target. Instead of the regulation 4¼-inch hole, practice putting to a 3½-inch hole or circle. Reducing the target will help you refine your putting touch and give you more confidence when you're putting to the regulation hole.

—*Chuck Hogan*

Toss the ball to develop putting 'feel'

Good putters seem to have a "feel" for distance.

How do you develop this skill? One technique is to lay aside the putter and practice tossing the ball to the hole underhanded.

You'll find that, the farther away you are, the more fully the arm must be extended toward the cup. The same principle applies with the putter. The farther the putter is extended toward the hole, the farther the ball will travel.

—*Ralph Bernhisel*

Drop a ball to get your eyes on line

Positioning your eyes over the target line is critical to aiming a putt properly. Many players are unaware that they set up with their eyes back from the line. The fault leads to confusion when you turn your head to confirm the position of the hole in preparation for making your stroke. To insure that your eyes are over the line, try this drill: Take your normal stance over the ball and then hold a second ball over your left eye. Drop the second ball. If you're set up properly, it should fall on top of the ball you are putting or just behind it.

—*Gus Novotny*

Strike down and hold to crispen your chip shots

When practicing chip shots, I recommend placing a range basket or golf bag or some other similar item about a yard in front of the ball. You'll soon discover that the way to hit the ball over the obstacle consistently is not with a scooping stroke. You'll learn to sharpen your contact and get the ball up quicker by striking down and through the ball. Feel that you're controlling the force of the swing with the left arm and hand. Don't allow the left wrist to collapse before or after impact. Strike down and hold with the left wrist staying firm. Then, try to duplicate this strike-and-hold action on the course.

—*Steve Adams*

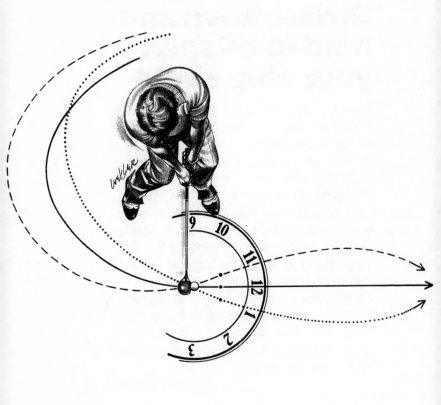

Use a second tee to dial the curve of your shots

To hit a slice, your swing path should move out-to-in across the target line. To hit a hook, it should move in-to-out. Cutting across the ball imparts a sidespin that causes curvature in flight. To hit the ball straight, the swing path should move along the target line through impact.

You can "dial" the desired swing path by placing a tee about five or six inches in front of the ball to act as a guide. For a straight shot, place the tee directly in front of your ball along the target line. For a slice, place it inside the target line, in an 11 o'clock position. For a hook, place it outside your target line, in a 1 o'clock position. Consider the tee as an intermediate target and try to swing through the ball along that line. This drill is only for practice—an extra tee when playing is against the rules.

—*John Hessey*

Cover ball with cup to eliminate tension

Learn to overcome the tendency to hit *at* rather than *through* the ball with this simple practice drill. Tee your ball as you would normally for a driver, then cover the ball with a large paper cup. Address the cup as you would a regular tee shot and swing. You'll find that the ball bursts through the paper cup and maintains a fairly normal trajectory.

Then when you get out on the golf course in a pressure situation, visualize a paper cup over your ball before tension sets in, and swing through the shot.
—*Warren Orlick*

12 JUNIORS

A collection of lessons to help young and beginning golfers improve their fundamentals and coordination. You don't have to be a kid to try them.

b.c.morse

Throw a ball for proper use of right arm

Most young golfers would benefit from learning to use their right arm and hand correctly in the golf swing—that is, swinging down and through the ball from inside to along the target line and releasing (turning the right hand over the left) just after impact. A handy drill you can perform anywhere requires only a ball of some type.

Holding the ball in your right hand, set up as if you were going to hit a golf shot, but position your club so the clubhead rests on the ground where a golf ball would be. Now imagine a dotted line on the ground from the clubhead to your target. With your right hand, toss the ball underhand *inside* the clubshaft but to the *right* of the imaginary dotted line. Throw the ball with right-to-left spin to curve it back to the left. This is how you want your right hand and arm performing in the golf swing.

—*Hank Johnson*

b.c.morse

Try the knees drill to develop an 'inside' swing path

A good drill for improving your swing is to hit practice shots on the range with your driver while kneeling. Many youngsters use their shoulders too much in their swings because they lack strength in their hands and arms. With the ball teed high, this knees drill helps give you better clubhead feel and the right blend of arm swing and wrist cock while reducing the overactivity of the shoulders. You may mis-hit—or even miss completely—the ball a few times at first, but keep trying the drill. Your regular shots should improve because the knees drill will help you swing on an inside path, which is the correct angle of approach for hitting the ball.

—*Jim Flick*

Weight forward, ball back for better chipping

A chip is a low, running shot that you should use when you are a few feet off the green and you have no obstacles between you and the pin. It's a shot you can practice in your backyard.

Using a 7-iron, set up to the ball with your weight more on your forward foot (the left foot for right-handers), the ball toward your other foot and your hands slightly ahead of the ball. Use the club as though it were a pendulum—swing your arms smoothly with minimal wristiness. You don't want a great deal of follow-through, so try to feel like all you are doing is tapping down on the back of the ball, with the clubhead swinging from high to low on the down-swing. The ball will fly relatively low, then will roll to the hole.

Practice to develop a feel for how long a swing you should make to send the ball different distances.

—*Sally Slater*

Roll a tennis ball for smoother takeaway

To insure a smooth, low, well-paced takeaway, take a tennis ball to your next practice session. Assume your address position, and place the tennis ball behind the clubhead. Feel the left arm and club roll the tennis ball away as you start your swing. A light, even grip pressure will allow the ball to hug the back of the club. You should soon feel your arms swinging back low and wide, which will result in a properly completed backswing and weight shift. Thinking of this drill will help when you play on the golf course.

—*Tom Ness*

Take a wastebasket and lay it on its side or prop it up at any angle. From various distances practice chipping shots into the basket.

Grab a bunch of golf balls and try juggling them. How many balls can you toss in the air without dropping them?

Bounce a golf ball repeatedly off the front of a wedge. How many times can you hit the ball without missing it?

Improve your hand-eye coordination

Playing sports besides golf is a very good way to improve your hand-eye coordination, which is essential if you want to play better golf. How efficiently your hands work with your eyes is a skill that most people take for granted.

Fortunately, there is a variety of sports, such as basketball, baseball and hockey, that can help you become a better all-round athlete. Remember, the more sports you participate in, the better your hand-eye coordination will be and the more fun you'll have.

You can improve your hand-eye ability outside or at home any time of year by practicing these three drills. Remember to practice them in a place where you won't break any glass, like your garage or basement.

—*John Elliott*

Swing low for solid contact

For the best iron shots, swing the club-head into the ball on the same low angle that it took at the start of the backswing. This should result in a shallow divot in front of the ball's original position. Many young golfers hear that they must hit down on the ball, so they swing the clubhead on an angle too steep or abrupt, and there is little chance of solidly hitting the back of the ball. But if the clubhead follows a low angle in the impact area, you will make sweet contact more often.

—*Davis Love*

Make putting practice fun

All great golfers have one thing in common: they all putt exceptionally well. As junior players, they all spent a great deal of their practice time putting.

Putting practice can be fun. See how many putts you can make in a row from one putter-length away, then two putter-lengths, then three. Keep track of your record from each distance.

Also practice longer putts. Putt 10 times from a given distance. Give yourself two points for each putt you sink and one point for each putt that finishes past the hole but within one putter-length of it. Once you make 10 or more points in 10 tries, repeat the process from farther away.

And compete with a friend on the putting green whenever you can. This makes practicing even more fun and sharpens your ability to putt well under pressure.

—*Dick Aultman*

Use three extra balls for more accurate chips

When chipping with a lofted club such as an 8-iron or pitching wedge, you should strike a *downward* blow with the club. This is best accomplished by placing the ball back in your stance and leaning your weight on your left foot. When you do this properly your hands will be forward—near your left thigh or knee.

A swinging motion with the arms from this position will cause your club to swing more up on the backswing and down on the forward swing. The combination of club loft and downward swing will cause the ball to pop in the air, travel on a direct trajectory and run to the hole.

A good practice drill is to place three balls in a semicircle about eight to 10 inches behind your ball. With your weight left, practice striking your ball without striking the other three balls.

—*Jack Lumpkin*

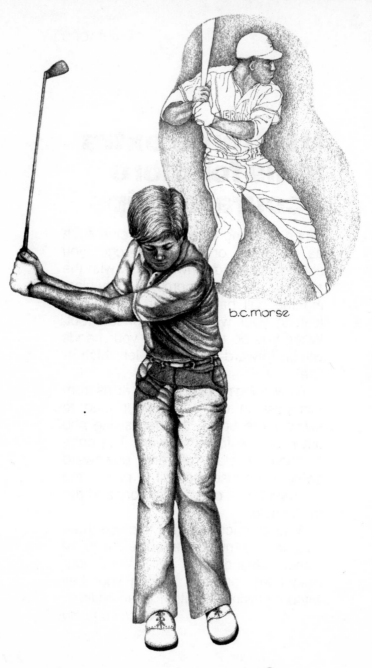

b.c.morse

Stride like a major-leaguer for effective weight shift

To learn the correct weight shift and the proper timing between your upper body and lower body, try this drill. Begin with your normal address position. Use a medium iron and put the ball on a tee. Now move your left foot next to your right foot, moving the clubhead back the same distance. From there, swing the club back normally. Then, as you swing forward, move your left foot to the left and put it where it started as you swing through the ball. This baseball "stride" will help you feel the proper movement of the upper and lower body throughout your normal swing.

—Peter Kostis

Right hand only

Left hand only

Use two hands to improve strength, swing

Golf is a two-handed game. For most golfers one arm shouldn't be dominant over the other—both arms need to work together to produce a consistent, free-flowing swing. To teach both of your arms to complement each other, do this drill 10 or 15 minutes a day:

First, with the ball teed and with a 5-, 7-, or 9-iron, hit a few shots with *just your right hand* gripping the club. Put your left hand in your pocket or behind your back so it's out of the way. Just try to make contact with the ball—don't swing too hard or fast.

Then repeat this drill but with *only your left hand* on the club. Don't worry about where the ball goes. After five or six shots with just the left hand on the club, alternate hitting one shot with only the right hand, one with only the left, then one with *both* hands gripping the club.

—*Bob Toski*

Better balance for better results

Balance is essential to consistent, well-struck shots. Many young players, however, lose their balance during the swing. One way to maintain good balance throughout the swing is to think of keeping your eyes on the ball until the clubhead makes contact. You shouldn't overdo this, though, because on the course your target should be your main thought when you swing. But watching the ball until impact—trying to see the clubface actually contacting the ball—will improve your balance and therefore your shots.

—*Paul Runyan*